WORLD ABOUT US

THE
GREENHOUSE
EFFECT

M. BRIGHT

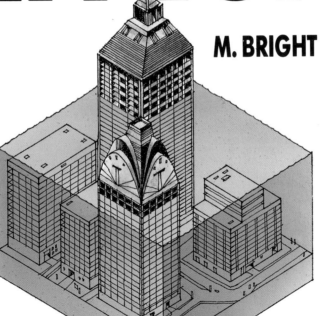

GLOUCESTER PRESS
London·New York·Toronto·Sydney·

© Aladdin Books 1991

Designed and produced by
Aladdin Books Ltd
28 Percy Street
London W1P 9FF

First published in
Great Britain in 1991 by
Franklin Watts Ltd
96 Leonard Street
London EC2A 4RH

Design: David West
Children's
Book Design
Editor: Fiona Robertson
Illustrator: Simon Bishop
Consultant: Brian Gardiner

ISBN 0 7496 0494 8

Printed in Belgium
All rights reserved

A CIP catalogue record for this
book is available from the
British Library.

Contents

Introduction

The conditions on Earth are just right for life. The Earth is kept warm by the heat from the Sun, and the atmosphere controls the Earth's temperature. This relationship between the Earth and the atmosphere is called the Greenhouse Effect. However, it is now under threat. The atmosphere is being polluted with gases that trap more heat from the Earth. This could lead to rising temperatures – or global warming.

The Greenhouse Effect

The layer of gases which surrounds the Earth is called the atmosphere. Energy from the Sun passes through the atmosphere and warms the Earth. The Earth's surface then gives off heat, some of which is absorbed by gases in the atmosphere. These gases stop some of the heat from escaping into space. This is rather like the way the glass in a greenhouse works, and so it is called the Greenhouse Effect.

The temperature inside a greenhouse can be kept much higher than that outside.

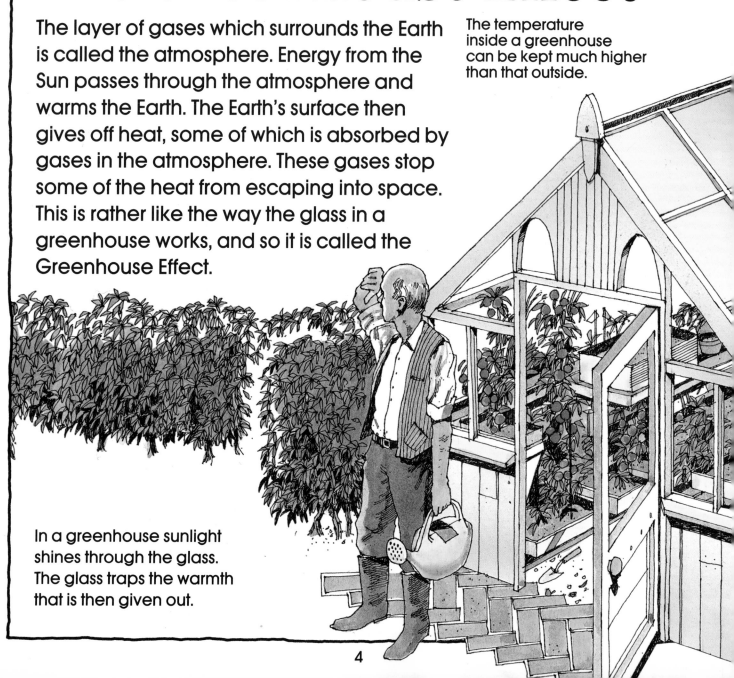

In a greenhouse sunlight shines through the glass. The glass traps the warmth that is then given out.

As a greenhouse provides the ideal conditions for many plants to flourish, so the atmosphere allows life on Earth to thrive.

Natural causes

The atmosphere contains a number of gases, often in tiny amounts, which trap the heat given out by the Earth. These are called greenhouse gases. Carbon dioxide, water vapour, methane, nitrous oxide and ozone are produced naturally on Earth, and are important greenhouse gases. In order to ensure that the Earth's temperature remains constant, the balance of these gases in the atmosphere must not be upset.

Water vapour is an important greenhouse gas.

Cattle produce methane during digestion.

Ozone can also be harmful at surface level.

Methane also comes from wet or swampy areas.

People and animals give out carbon dioxide when they breathe.

When plant material is broken down in the soil, nitrous oxide is produced.

Volcanoes also produce carbon dioxide.

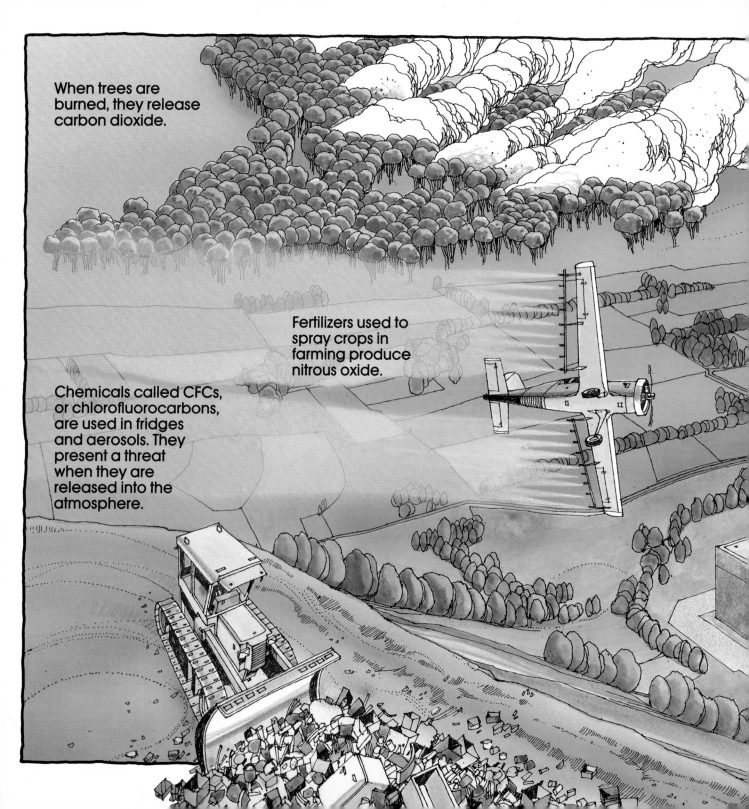

When trees are burned, they release carbon dioxide.

Fertilizers used to spray crops in farming produce nitrous oxide.

Chemicals called CFCs, or chlorofluorocarbons, are used in fridges and aerosols. They present a threat when they are released into the atmosphere.

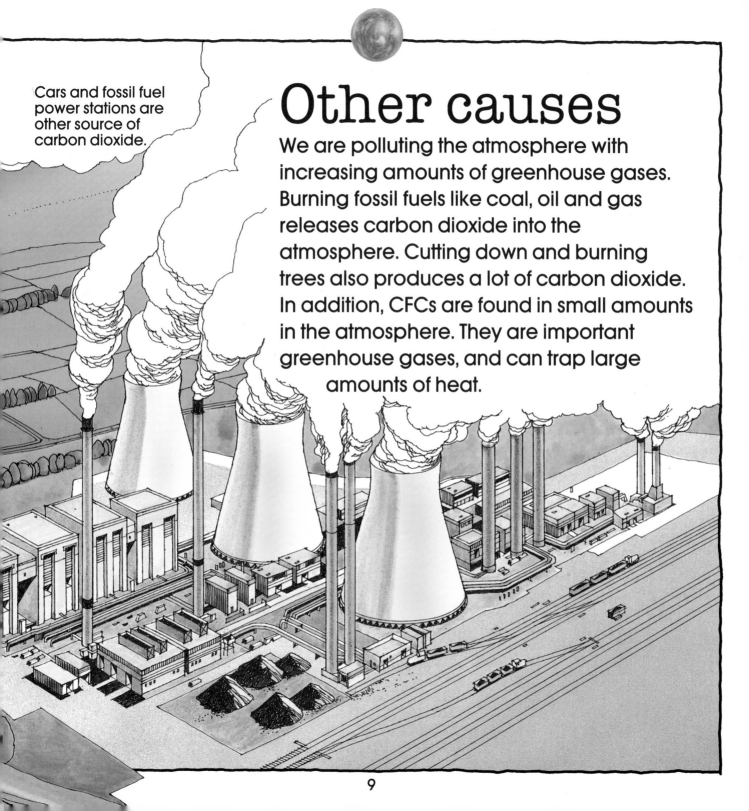

Cars and fossil fuel power stations are other source of carbon dioxide.

Other causes

We are polluting the atmosphere with increasing amounts of greenhouse gases. Burning fossil fuels like coal, oil and gas releases carbon dioxide into the atmosphere. Cutting down and burning trees also produces a lot of carbon dioxide. In addition, CFCs are found in small amounts in the atmosphere. They are important greenhouse gases, and can trap large amounts of heat.

The effects

A rise of a few degrees in the Earth's temperatures could make huge differences to conditions around the world. Temperatures in Britain could become like those in Mediterranean countries, such as Greece and Spain. Countries will have to grow different crops according to the changes in their weather. In the Arctic and Antarctic, the polar ice may start to melt.

The bright surface of the ice caps reflects sunlight away from the Earth. But if the ice caps melt, more land will be uncovered which will absorb more heat.

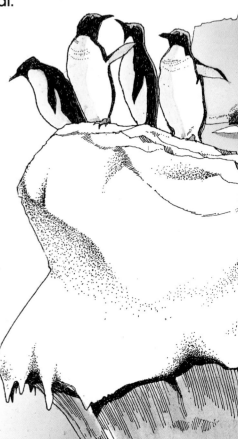

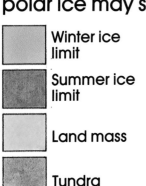

Winter ice limit

Summer ice limit

Land mass

Tundra

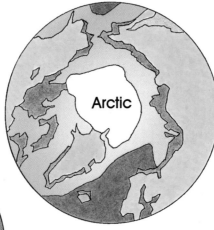

Arctic

Antarctic

This maps shows the amount of ice in the Arctic and Antarctic at different times of the year.

Penguins and seals
may be threatened
if the polar ice melts.

Rising sea levels

Ice melting in the Antarctic and Greenland will flow into the sea. All over the world sea levels may rise, perhaps by as much as 20 to 40 cm by the beginning of the next century. Low-lying areas, like Bangladesh and the Netherlands, will be covered with saltwater. The crops and the land will be ruined. Places near the sea, such as parts of Florida, would also be flooded.

The Dutch polders are areas of land that have been reclaimed from the sea. They are now used for growing crops on.

Flood barriers, like the Thames Barrier in London, can be raised to act against high sea levels. They reduce the risk of flooding.

The pattern of tropical storms and hurricanes could change.

Former agricultural areas become dry, barren dust bowls.

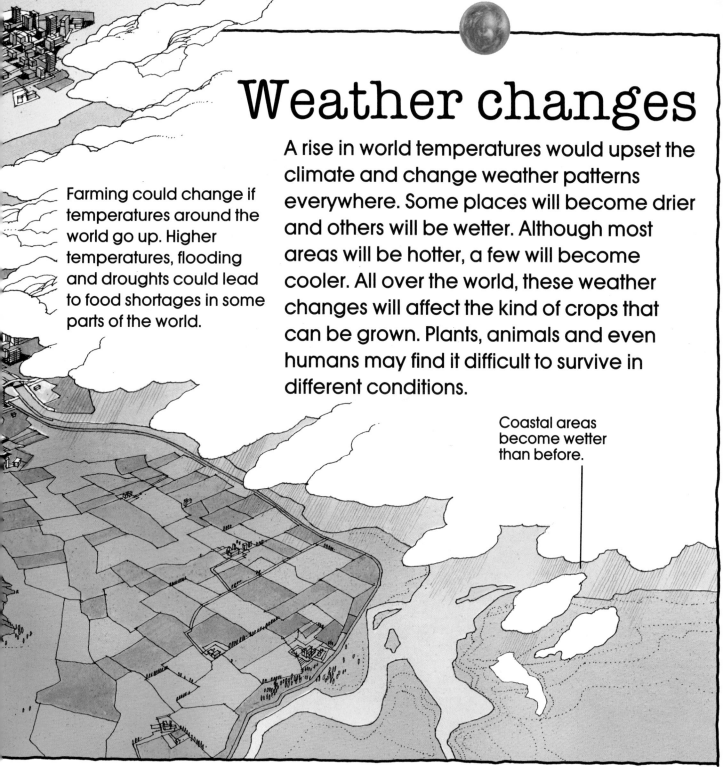

Weather changes

A rise in world temperatures would upset the climate and change weather patterns everywhere. Some places will become drier and others will be wetter. Although most areas will be hotter, a few will become cooler. All over the world, these weather changes will affect the kind of crops that can be grown. Plants, animals and even humans may find it difficult to survive in different conditions.

Farming could change if temperatures around the world go up. Higher temperatures, flooding and droughts could lead to food shortages in some parts of the world.

Coastal areas become wetter than before.

In danger

As climate and weather patterns alter, the homes of plants and animals all over the world will change. If the ice in the Arctic melts, polar bears and seals will have to find new hunting grounds. Elsewhere, as sea levels rise, other plants and animals will also be threatened. If saltmarshes and estuaries disappear, many wading birds will be homeless.

Rising temperatures and melting ice will affect ocean currents too. Seas rich with food and life could become barren and lifeless.

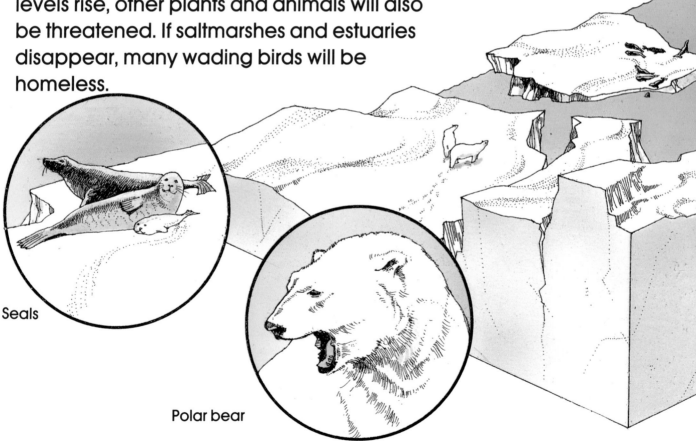

Seals

Polar bear

Plants in saltmarshes

Plants and animals have taken millions of years to get used to the conditions in one place. If these conditions change, many of them, like the mole (shown right) would find it difficult to survive.

The first victims

A warming of the oceans would affect many animals living in or near the sea, like penguins, whales and seals. North Sea seals gather at breeding sites during warm weather. However, unusually long warm periods recently meant they remained crowded together for longer. Diseases spread more easily. Many animals died, perhaps the first victims of global warming. Many other land animals could also suffer.

Polar bear

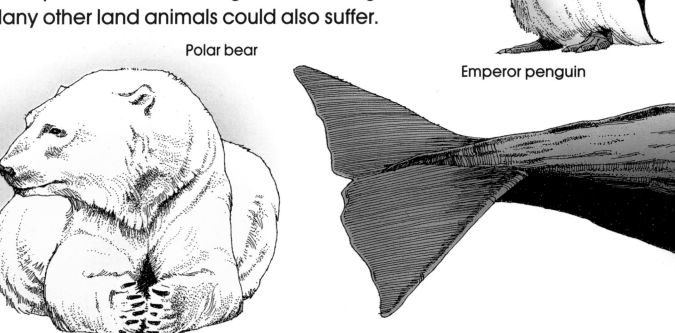

Emperor penguin

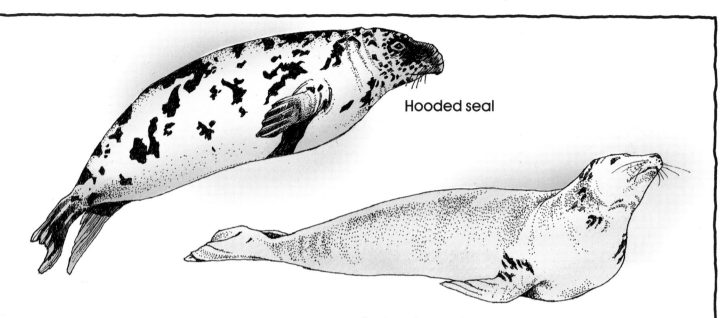

Hooded seal

Crabeater seal

Sperm whale

The evidence

Weather stations all over the world have been recording a gradual rise in the temperature of the air. They have also found an increase in the amounts of carbon dioxide and other greenhouse gases found in the atmosphere. During the 1980s, the world had six of the hottest years ever recorded. Such weather changes are thought to be caused by the increase in pollution from power stations and cars.

Scientists in Hawaii have been measuring the amount of carbon dioxide in the air for more than 30 years. By using lasers their results are very accurate. In Greenland, they drill deep into the ice and take samples that have been trapped for many years.

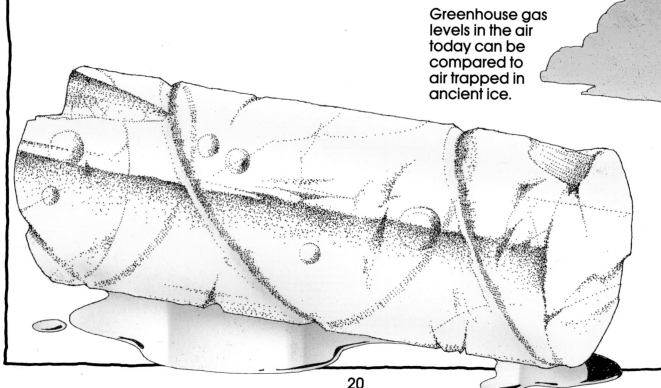

Greenhouse gas levels in the air today can be compared to air trapped in ancient ice.

21

Natural controls

All over the Earth, plants, from tiny plankton in the sea to the huge trees in the forests, take in carbon dioxide and give out oxygen. This means that there is lots of oxygen in the air for humans and animals to breathe. But when plants die, they give back their carbon dioxide to the atmosphere. New plants must be grown to use up this carbon dioxide. Otherwise, it will build up in the atmosphere.

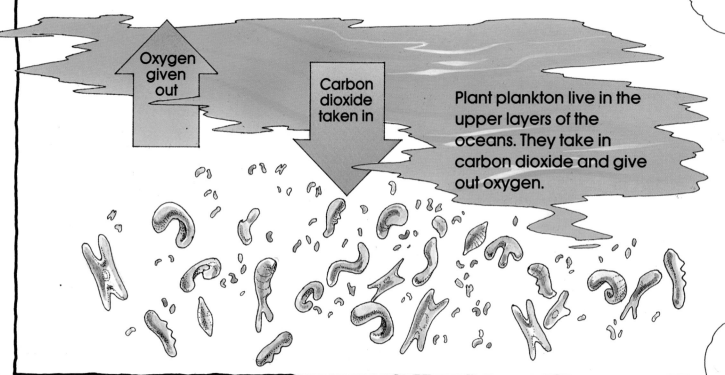

Oxygen given out

Carbon dioxide taken in

Plant plankton live in the upper layers of the oceans. They take in carbon dioxide and give out oxygen.

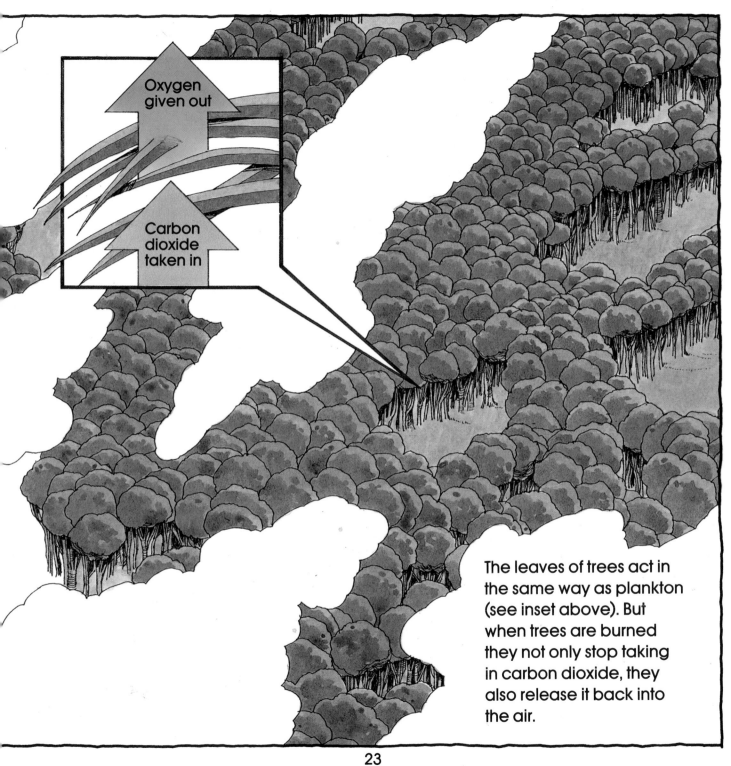

Oxygen
given out

Carbon
dioxide
taken in

The leaves of trees act in the same way as plankton (see inset above). But when trees are burned they not only stop taking in carbon dioxide, they also release it back into the air.

Venera probes landed on Venus and measured the amount of carbon dioxide in the atmosphere.

The surface of Venus has a temperature of 480°C. This makes it impossible for plants and animals to survive there.

Out of control

The balance of gases in the Earth's atmosphere allows conditions to be right for life. Too much carbon dioxide in the atmosphere could make the Earth overheat, and become like Venus. The surface of Venus is hidden by thick cloud and the atmosphere is made up mostly of carbon dioxide. This means that heat from the surface of the planet is trapped.

Putting it right

There are many things we can do to avoid the threat of global warming. We can use alternative sources of energy – wave, solar and wind power – that do not release carbon dioxide into the atmosphere. We can make our homes and factories more efficient so we use less energy. And we can replant forests which take in some carbon dioxide and stop it building up in the atmosphere.

Tidal power can be used in large estuaries.

Wave power uses the energy of the oceans.

Floating rafts can produce electricity from the motion of the waves.

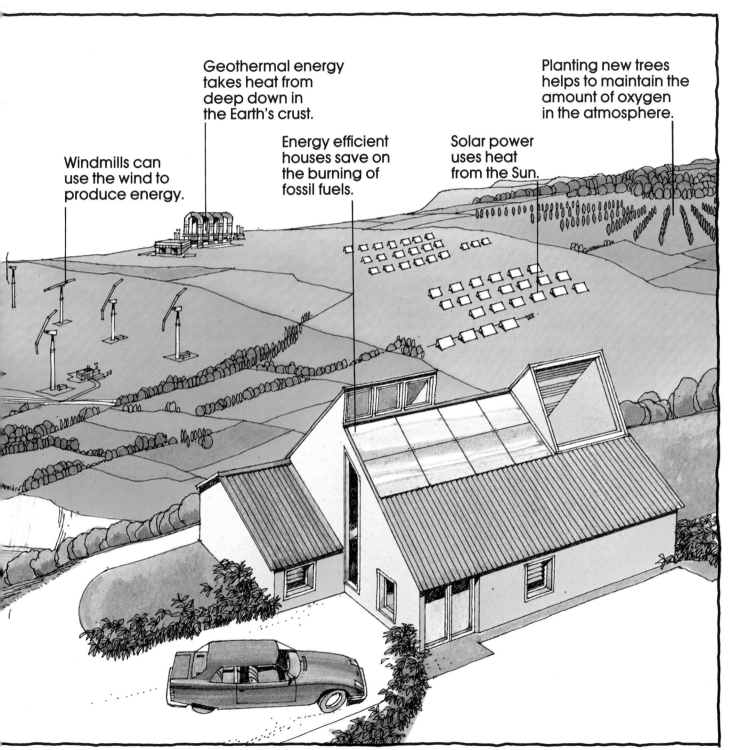

Geothermal energy takes heat from deep down in the Earth's crust.

Planting new trees helps to maintain the amount of oxygen in the atmosphere.

Energy efficient houses save on the burning of fossil fuels.

Solar power uses heat from the Sun.

Windmills can use the wind to produce energy.

Did you know?

If the average temperature all over the world rose by just 4°C, it has been calculated that the global sea level would be about five metres higher than it is today. Whole cities would disappear under water.

Polar ice is thick and old. By drilling out cores of ice, scientists can find out what gases were in the atmosphere long ago. In the 18th century, there was much less carbon dioxide than there is today.

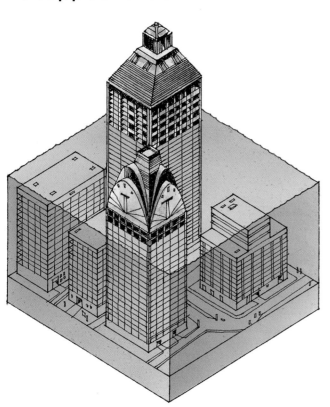

A 4°C rise in global temperature would melt a lot of polar ice. However, a 4°C drop in global temperature would plunge the planet into another Ice Age. This could lead to very cold conditions.

Even the plants that live in the ocean will be affected. Tiny plant plankton are at the bottom of the food chain. If they suffer from a warming of the oceans, this could affect many different kinds of other animals in the seas, from whales, to fish, to corals.

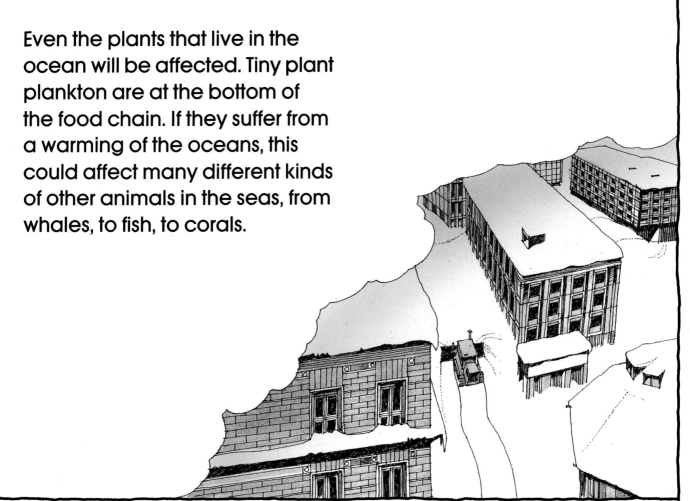

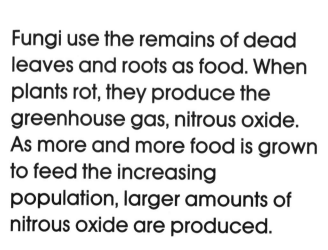

Even a warming of only 1°C in global temperature would reduce the amount of wheat harvested in North America and Central Asia. It would also change the climate in the rice-growing regions of the world. Wheat and rice are the two main food crops. If they suffer millions of people could starve.

Fungi use the remains of dead leaves and roots as food. When plants rot, they produce the greenhouse gas, nitrous oxide. As more and more food is grown to feed the increasing population, larger amounts of nitrous oxide are produced.

Glossary

Atmosphere
The layer of gases that surrounds and protects the Earth. It is about 700km thick.

CFCs /chlorofluorocarbons
Chemicals used in products like aerosols and fridges.

Global warming
Pollution has increased the Greenhouse Effect by putting more gases that trap heat into the atmosphere. This makes the Earth's temperatures go up, and is called global warming.

Greenhouse Effect
The normal process by which heat is kept in the atmosphere. Without it, life could not survive on Earth. But if too much heat is trapped, temperatures could go up. This would then be dangerous to life.

Greenhouse gases
The gases which trap the heat that comes from the Earth. Many of them occur naturally, like carbon dioxide and methane. Others, like CFCs, are caused by human actions.

Methane
A gas that is given out when bacteria break down plant and animal materials. Methane is a greenhouse gas.

Water vapour
An invisible gas in the atmosphere. It is made when water heats up and evaporates. Water vapour also helps to trap heat in the atmosphere.

Index

PRINTED IN BELGIUM BY

INTERNATIONAL BOOK PRODUCTION